HAMSTERS

Joyce Lawrence

Hamlyn

London · New York · Sydney · Toronto

Introduction

A single Golden Hamster and her litter were discovered near Aleppo, Syria in 1930, and it is from this one family that all pet Golden Hamsters are descended. The hamster was first introduced into the UK in 1931, but it was not until after the Second World War that its potential as a

The Golden Hamster makes an extremely attractive and interesting pet.

disease-free and amenable pet was recognized. It is now one of the most popular smaller mammals kept, with many colour variations having been developed. There are numerous clubs and societies, and shows and exhibitions have become commonplace.

While hamsters are now available in a range of colours, the normal Golden Hamster is still by far the most popular variety. An average adult is about 15cm (6in) in length. The fur is glossy and the skin is rather loose. The paws are good at grasping, and the hamster uses them both to grasp branches which it gnaws and to groom itself almost continually.

Like all rodents, the hamster must constantly gnaw wooden objects to prevent its incisor teeth growing too long. The animal's eyesight is rather poor, but its hearing is acute.

The animal's lifespan is relatively short, about 18-24 months, although many live less than a year. Cases of hamsters living for seven years, and in one case for 10 years, have been recorded but these are unusual.

A hamster is an excellent family pet, but it is not recommended for young children because they could have difficulty handling them, and the animal has a tendency to bite.

Hamsters are very nocturnal in their habits, being active in the evening, and so are good pets for people who are absent from the house during the day. The animal enjoys exercise and will constantly scamper around the cage playing with toys, storing food, making its bed, etc.

They are very easy to keep and are extremely clean if cared for properly, and can be housed in a much more confined space than many other small pets.

Choosing and buying a hamster

Unlike the rabbit, there are few breeds of hamsters to choose from. All domestic pets are descended from the Golden or Syrian Hamster (*Mesocricetus auratus*); the Common Hamster (*Cricetus cricetus*) is nearly twice as big and ranges throughout most of Europe. There are however a large variety of colours available. Albinos, creams, greys and piebalds are some of the colours that have been developed from the Golden Hamster imported from Syria, and both long and shorthaired varieties are available.

Hamsters should preferably be bought from pet shops

A clean nose, erect ears and clear, bright eyes are all signs of a healthy hamster.

or accredited suppliers where only good quality stock is kept. Hamsters are one of the few animals that should not be bought from the amateur breeder without careful investigation, as they may possibly be weakened from too much inbreeding using inferior stock.

Hamsters have a tendency to bite and so it is best to buy one at about 6-8 weeks of age so that it can be readily tamed. Hamsters unfortunately tend to fight if kept in groups, and even a breeding pair should not be housed together, except for mating.

It does not make a great deal of difference if your pet is male or female as lifespan and temperament are about the same.

When purchasing hamsters, a number of points should be checked, and the hamster's health should be examined carefully using the following list as a guide.

Signs of health

Head
Nose Clean, no discharge.
Eyes Clear and bright, no discharge.
Ears Erect and free from scabs and waxy discharge.
Teeth Growing parallel, not overlong

Body
Coat Should be glossy and well groomed, with no evidence of areas of hair loss, sores or wounds. Examine under the tail to ensure it is dry and clean.
Feet No missing or damaged claws.

Daytime drowsiness is of course normal as the animals are nocturnal. Faeces in the cage should be solid, well formed and dark brown in colour.

Colour and coat variations

All adult hamsters are about the same size and shape but there are now many differently coloured varieties which have been bred in captivity.

Golden Hamsters These are by far the most common type of hamster and are the ones most often seen in a pet shop. All the variations have black eyes but there are three shades of fur.

Normal Golden The coat is basically golden with dark tips to the hairs and greyish roots. The abdomen is white and the animal has dark grey ears.

Dark Golden There is a reddish sheen to the coat and the black tips to the hairs are much more pronounced. The ears are black.

Light Golden The black tips to the hairs are absent. The variation has a white abdomen.

Cream Hamsters Unlike the Golden Hamster, the coat colour is constant but the eyes are different. There are three different eye colours in this variation: Red-eyed Cream, Ruby-eyed Cream and Black-eyed Cream. The last was one of the earliest colours to be bred. This variety also has a deeper coloured coat than the other two varieties as well as darker ears.

Grey Hamsters Again there are three shades of Grey Hamster. They are all fairly new varieties.

Dominant Grey This variety has black eyes and ears. The coat is dark grey overlaid with flesh coloured tint.

Dark Grey This is dark grey overall with black ears and eyes.

Light Grey The distinctive red eyes in this variety make it easily recognizable. It has a silvery tinge to the coat.

The Dark Grey and Ruby-eyed
Cream are two of the colour variations available.

White (Albino) Hamsters There are two varieties of
Albino Hamsters as well as a White Hamster.
Albino This is completely white with pink eyes.
Dark-eared Albino As the name suggests, it is the same as
the Albino but with dark ears.
Black-eyed White The coat is white and there are black
eyes and pink ears.
Other colours
Cinnamon This is the brightest hamster with a rich
orange fur and lighter ears.
Yellow This is similar to the Black-eyed Cream but the fur
is slightly darker with darker guard hairs, which the
cream does not have.

Honey This variety resembles the Yellow, but there are red eyes and lighter ears.

Rust The fur is darker than the Cinnamon and there are black eyes and brown ears.

Sepia Although sometimes confused with the Grey Hamster, they are in fact more beige than grey. The eyes are black and the ears grey.

Smoke Pearl The coat is completely pearl grey, the eyes are black and the ears are dark grey.

Blond The fur is blond and the eyes are red.

Dove The fur is medium grey with dark bases; the

A Tortoiseshell and White Hamster (below) and a Cinnamon Hamster (bottom).

abdomen is white. The eyes are black with dark grey ears.

Marked colours

Banded These hamsters have an unbroken band of white circling the body. The fur can be any colour, and examples are the Light-grey Banded, Cinnamon Banded and the Cream Banded.

Piebald The Piebald Hamsters is basically white with patches of colour rather like the piebald horse. Piebald Hamsters tend to be smaller than normal and the females do not make good mothers.

Dominant Spot This variety has begun to replace the Piebald Hamster as the markings are very similar, but the hamsters are not undersized and the females make good mothers.

Tortoiseshell and White These hamsters are very similar in pattern to the tortoiseshell cat. The coat is overlaid with golden and white patches. There is also a banded variety of this hamster. There are also Cinnamon Tortoiseshells and Grey Tortoiseshells but the colour contrast is less than in the white.

Coat varieties Most hamsters are shorthaired varieties, but there are three other main fur types.

Satin This is very similar to the shorthaired but the coat has a glossy sheen which makes the colours look much richer.

Longhaired The coat is long, fine and dense. This type of coat needs to be groomed regularly as it tends to become tangled.

Rex The coat of the Rex is in a class of its own, being long, dense and curly. The young hamsters have a wavy coat. The whiskers are also curled.

Housing

This is a basic hamster cage with a solid-backed exercise wheel and a nesting box.

Cages Hamsters are rodents and need to gnaw constantly to keep their teeth from becoming overgrown. Any housing must be able to withstand constant gnawing. An appropriate size is 60cm x 30cm x 20cm (24in x 12in x 8in). If made of wood it should be plywood or hardwood at least 12mm ($\frac{1}{2}$in) thick with all exposed edges covered with a metal strip.

Commercially available hamster cages are usually made from metal or plastic. A recent alternative to the conventional hamster cage is the Rotastak system which can be extended to mimic the complex set of burrows which the wild hamster would occupy.

Hamster cages are also available in the shape of 'space stations' and bird cages. A glass aquarium with a well-fitting wire top can make an ideal home for a hamster. Choose one with a floor area of at least 1250 sq cm (200 sq in).

Accessories If food and water bowls are to be used they should be of a non-tip earthenware type although water bottles and hopper-type food containers are preferable.

Exercise wheel Hamsters may spend many hours in an exercise wheel and will probably run miles in a day. Never use spoked wheels, as after only one

A more elaborate form of housing is the Rotastak system. Different modules may be combined to mimic the complex system of burrows which hamsters occupy in the wild.

slip the hamster could end up with a broken leg. Always purchase exercise wheels with a solid back.

Hamster playballs A recent introduction is the hamster playball. This is a plastic sphere in which the hamster is placed. The animal must become accustomed to the ball by being placed in it for no more than a few minutes

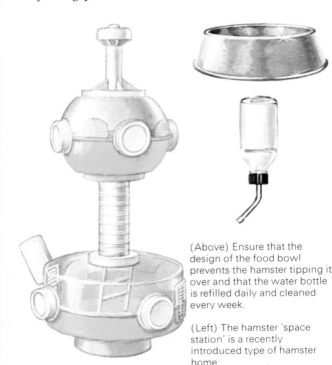

(Above) Ensure that the design of the food bowl prevents the hamster tipping it over and that the water bottle is refilled daily and cleaned every week.

(Left) The hamster 'space station' is a recently introduced type of hamster home.

A variety of playthings, such as cardboard tubes, cotton reels and jam jars, will prevent your pet becoming bored.

initially. The time can be gradually increased up to 20 minutes in any hour. This will allow the hamster free access to your home without the fear of it escaping or causing damage. The hamster must be supervised at all times while in the playball.

Cage accessories Ladders and branches can be placed in the cage for climbing into the nest box normally provided in the commercial hamster cage. Wooden objects and twigs should also be provided for the hamster to chew on such as pieces of soft wood, branches of apple, blackthorn, hawthorn or willow, cotton reels and nuts. This will keep the hamster's teeth in good condition and perhaps prevent it from gnawing the cage.

13

Handling

Hamsters are very nervous and easily frightened when young, so cage cleaning and initial handling should be done very quietly and as gently as possible, with no sudden movements. Confidence is essential when handling hamsters but this will only come with practice and you must expect the occasional nip before you gain your hamster's trust.

When handling a new hamster for the first time, allow it to smell your hands before attempting to pick it up. Use this opportunity to offer titbits and to stroke the animal. Initially, handle the hamster by scooping it up and allowing it to sit in the cupped hands. When the hamster has become used to being handled in this way, begin to pick it up with the palm of the hand over the body (the

Scoop up your hamster and allow it to sit in your cupped hands.

Only pick up hamsters in this way when they have become used to being handled.

hamster's head facing towards the wrist), closing the fingers around the hamster's abdomen. Hold firmly but do not squeeze. Never disturb sleeping hamsters as they will resent this and will bite.

Children and hamsters Children under eight years old should not be encouraged to handle hamsters. Inept handling leads to a bite, and once a hamster has a grip on a finger, it may be reluctant to let go. A bad experience such as this for a young child could colour his or her attitude to pets for the rest of his or her life. All children should be encouraged to sit on the floor whilst playing with a hamster. A hamster dropped from a height is usually a dead hamster.

General management

The floor of the cage should be covered with layers of newspaper topped with a 2·5cm (1in) layer of sawdust and wood shavings; other possible flooring materials are peat, cat litter or zeolite (a natural resin).

Nesting materials have proved troublesome with the exception of the shredded paper based beddings and the recently introduced artificial fur-bedding. Long stranded man-made synthetic materials can kill hamsters because they are indigestible and become impacted in the intestines; trapping, with subsequent loss or injury to the limbs, is also common. Many people still prefer to

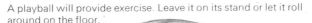

A playball will provide exercise. Leave it on its stand or let it roll around on the floor.

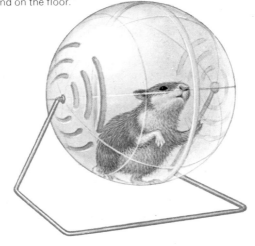

provide more natural products such as hay, but this must be short-chopped and dust-free.

Hamsters are clean animals and usually urinate in the same part of the cage, but they will produce a strong smell unless the cage is cleaned out regularly. The sawdust from this area should be removed daily and the cage completely cleaned out once a week. Clean parts of the old bedding should be mixed with the new bedding so that the hamster returns to a familiar smell. Hamsters can soon be taught to urinate in one place. If a shallow tray containing cat litter is placed in one corner of the cage, topped with a small amount of soiled litter, it will encourage the hamster to use this 'toilet'.

Hamsters should be kept indoors except during the hottest summer days when the cage can be placed outdoors, but it should be kept out of direct sunlight and protected from cats. It is particularly important in winter to ensure an equitable temperature at night because hamsters can become dormant and even appear dead below 4°C (40°F). Any apparently dead hamster under these circumstances should be placed somewhere warm, this has resurrected many 'dead' hamsters.

Food should be stored in sealable plastic containers and only small quantities should be bought at a time to prevent it becoming stale before use.

Hamsters enjoy leaving their cage for exercise and whilst the tabletop is an ideal playground it must be closely supervised to prevent any injuries from falls. Leaving hamsters on the floor to exercise can lead to their disappearance into the skirting board or floor boards, etc. A hamster playball will provide floor exercise without the likelihood of escape.

Feeding

Hoarding Your hamster should be fed once a day and the best time is in the evening when he is becoming active. 'Hamster' comes from the German word *hamstern* meaning 'to hoard', and hoarding food is a characteristic of these small rodents. A hamster will rarely consume all his food at one time but will store part of the meal and

Hamsters need green food in their diet, and clover (left) and dandelion (right) are both acceptable.

return to it at intervals during the day. To carry his food around, the hamster has two large cheek pouches which can be packed with food. These pouches are emptied into the food stores which may be located in a number of places within the cage, including the sleeping quarters. Because of this storing habit, food that will sour rapidly if stored should be removed regularly. This habit, however, can be used to advantage if you go away for a few days when the stored food will be drawn upon when the hamster is hungry.

Diet An adult hamster needs about 15g ($\frac{1}{2}$oz) of food daily as well as access to a supply of drinking water.

A basic balanced diet is easily obtained from your local pet shop or you can make it up yourself with assorted grains including flaked and whole maize, assorted birdseed, broken dog biscuits and rabbit pellets. Whilst hamsters are very fond of sunflower seeds, they should be provided only in small numbers because of their high oil content. Stale bread and cakes, crusts and biscuits may also be fed, and can be stored by the hamster for some time without deteriorating.

Greens and fruit Fresh greens and fruit are also essentials in the make-up of the hamster's diet. Cabbage, kale, lettuce and water cress will be eaten with relish as will slices of apple, carrot, swede and turnip. All of the latter groups are a useful source of winter food when greens are scarce and expensive. Raisins are also palatable.

Wild plants Certain species of wild plants can also be fed to your pet. These include chickweed, clover, coltsfoot, cow parsley, dandelion, docks, groundsel, plaintain, sorrel, vetches and fresh grasses. Green food must be well washed and dried before use and only small quantities

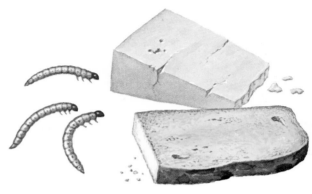

Mealworms, cheese and toast are all tasty treats, but should be given only occasionally.

should be offered at a time.

Weeds that are poisonous and should be avoided include bindweed, buttercup, hemlock, ragwort and speedwell.

No plants should be offered to your pet that are likely to have been sprayed with pesticide or that have been collected from the verges of roads as lead contamination from exhaust fumes is likely.

Titbits Cheese, plain potato crisps, hamster hoops, mealworms, caterpillars, moths and earthworms may be offered as titbits and are normally eaten avidly. They should, however, be offered as occasional treats, rather than as regular additions to the diet or digestive upsets might occur. Sweets and chocolates should never be given, because they clog the cheek pouches (see page 27).

Drink Water should always be available for the hamster to drink in a non-tip container or preferably in a gravity-feed bottle, which avoids contamination of the water with food and faeces. Water should be changed daily with the bottle being cleaned and sterilized at least twice weekly.

Small quantities of milk are enjoyed by hamsters. However, this should be removed if not drunk within a reasonable time. If the milk is left in the cage too long it will go sour, and if then drunk could cause digestive upsets.

Hamsters gnaw their food and store it in their cheek pouches before carrying it to food stores hidden in their cages.

Breeding

Sexing hamsters
Cubs Until they are 8-10 days old, young female hamsters may be identified by their having two rows of seven nipples on the abdomen. Very soon afterwards the fur will have grown sufficiently dense for these to be totally concealed.
Adults The sexing of adults is relatively easy. The male has an elongated rear end, the female is more rounded. The genital openings in males are twice as far apart as those in the female. In adult males, the testicles become very pronounced forming a pair of bulges at the base of the tail.
Mating Hamsters are prolific breeders capable of producing litters throughout the year, although there are fewer cubs in the litters during the winter. However,

Sexing adult hamsters is easy: look for a more elongated rear in the male and a more rounded one in the female.

male   female

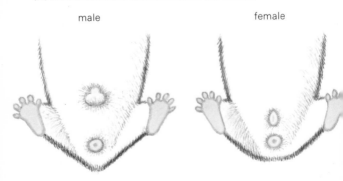

When they are ready to mate, the male will approach the female from behind while she stands still and looks straight ahead.

they are solitary by nature and should be kept in separate cages from six weeks of age to prevent possible fatal fighting as well as unwanted pregnancies.

Hamsters can breed for the first time at about 8 weeks of age although it is usual to delay the first mating until at least the age of 12 weeks.

Males will mate at any time and females come into season every four days. The most obvious sign is a slight swelling and reddening of the vaginal opening. The female is introduced into the male's cage in the evening, this being the time when she is likely to be most receptive. (*Never* introduce the male into the female's cage as she will almost certainly attack him.)

If the female is ready to be mated, she will 'freeze' into an unmistakable posture. She will crouch forward with

The size of a litter is normally 2-8, but litters of up to 16 have been recorded.

the head, body and hind limbs stretched out and with the tail raised. They will usually mate several times in quick succession, after which the female should be removed.

To be certain of a successful mating, the female must be put into the male's cage on four successive evenings. Some authors recommend that they should be left together overnight but this leads to unnecessary fights and injuries. A period of 20 minutes together is probably

24

a sufficient length of time.

Pregnancy The period of pregnancy varies from 15-18 days with most litters being produced 16 days after mating. This is the briefest gestation period of any mammal. By the middle of the second week after mating, the female will be showing obvious signs of pregnancy. During this week the bedding should be replaced and extra amounts supplied so that she can build a nest. The female will need additional protein and vitamins during the second half of pregnancy and while suckling the cubs. Fresh water must always be available with the bottle or bowl being topped up twice daily during the period the mother is suckling her young.

The nest should not be disturbed unnecessarily after the cubs have been born as this might endanger them. Litters vary in size from 2-8 but litters of up to 16 have been known to be produced. When born, the cubs are about 3cm (1in) in length and are completely helpless, being born blind and hairless.

Rearing the young For the first week, the cubs will only consume their mother's milk. Their eyes open after 5-7 days and a reasonable coat of hair has grown by the end of the week. By this time the cubs will start to eat solid food which has been hoarded by the mother, and will start eating finely chopped greens from about 10 days of age.

They will be weaned by 25 days when the mother should be removed, and will each weigh about 25-40g (1-1½oz). Between 4-6 weeks the sexes should be separated to avoid mating.

The female can be mated again one month after giving birth, which is soon after the first litter has been weaned.

Diseases

If your hamster is ill, seek veterinary advice as soon as possible. With many of the diseases of hamsters, by the time the symptoms have been recognized it is too late for successful treatment. The importance of hygiene in the handling of hamsters can not be overstressed (see *Rules of Hygiene*). Anyone suffering from a cold or influenza should not handle a hamster as the infection can be passed on to the animal.

Rules of Hygiene
1 Wash your hands after handling the hamster or cleaning out the cage.
2 Wash the hamster's food dishes and water bottle separately from the household crockery.
3 The hamster's food must be stored separately from the owner's food in sealable containers to prevent access by vermin.
4 Animals must not be brought into or be allowed onto work surfaces within food preparation or food storage areas or kitchens.
5 Never eat or drink whilst playing with a hamster or when cleaning out a cage.
6 Young children must be supervised to ensure that these rules are kept.

Ailments
Cage paralysis This distressing condition can be caused when there is little space available for exercise. Always provide plenty of exercise opportunities for the hamster such as an exercise wheel.

Cannibalism Female hamsters occasionally eat their cubs either because of disturbance or lack of milk. Piebald hamsters are likely to eat their young unless given absolute privacy after birth.

Cheek pouches Whole oats or barley in husks should be avoided in the food. The husks have sharp tips that can damage the lining of the pouches. Sticky foods such as chocolate can become impacted in the pouches, and this leads to infection. The pouches must be washed out with water after being manually emptied by the hamster's owner.

Common cold Symptoms include sneezing and a sore and runny nose and eyes. The animals must be kept warm, the nose clear and they should be encouraged to eat. Change the bedding frequently. There may be a connection between colds and influenza in man and in the hamster handled by them. Stay away from your hamster if you have a cold, and also make sure the cage is not damp or in a draught.

Constipation Young hamsters about two weeks old may become constipated if they do not have access to water. They develop a swollen abdomen and distended anus. If their cage has a water bottle, make certain that the young can reach it. Feeding dampened green stuffs may help to prevent this condition.

Lymphocytic choriomeningitis This is a serious disease of hamsters that can be transmitted to humans. A hamster suffering from it will be very obviously ill, and must be taken to the vet. Hamsters bought from an accredited source will be free of this disease.

Overgrown teeth Hamsters are rodents and as such their teeth grow continually. Supply plenty of material for the hamster to gnaw. Check the teeth regularly, if they become overgrown, take the hamster to the vet for them to be clipped short. Like humans, hamsters do not enjoy going to the dentist (see the illustration on page 29).

Paralysis As well as cage paralysis there are a number of similar ailments. Paralysis of the hind limbs affects males of certain strains aged between 6 and 10 months of age. This may be an inherited condition. Falls and Vitamin E deficiency are other common causes. The hamster should be taken to the vet.

Salmonellosis Affected hamsters lose weight and may develop diarrhoea. The infection can be spread to man and produce symptoms of food poisoning. Buy your hamster from accredited stock and wash your hands after handling or playing with your hamster.

Skin diseases In old age or in females recently weaned after large litters, patchy loss of hair and scaliness of the skin will occur. This is treated by improving the quality of the diet. Mange and ringworm can also cause hair loss but are usually associated with intense itching. These conditions can be transmitted to the owner.

Tapeworms Heavy infestations of tapeworms will cause diarrhoea which may contain mucous or blood. Live worms may be visible around the swollen and ulcerated anus. The affected animal will become lethargic and lose weight. Death can occur if the hamster does not receive veterinary treatment. Hamsters bought from an accredited source should be free of this disease.

Wet tail This disease is self explanatory. Diarrhoea causes a wet tail and the droppings are soft and watery rather than being firm and dry. However, in 'wet tail' the symptoms are worse and there is also a discharge around the tail. The disease is extremely contagious for other hamsters, but it is found mainly in the wild. Stress and infection usually combine to cause this disease when it does occur in pets. Only prompt attention by a vet is likely to be successful.

Broken bones and fractures The most common cause is a fall or a fight. No home treatment is possible; seek veterinary assistance immediately.

All rodents including the hamster have a pair of incisor teeth at the front separated from the cheek teeth by a small gap. The incisors grow constantly and your hamster will gnaw hard objects continually to keep them short. If the incisors grow too long, take your hamster to the vet for treatment.

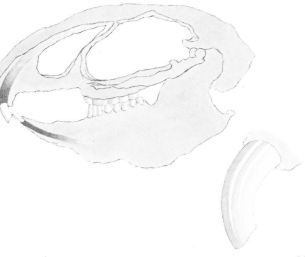

29

Exhibiting

Although a hamster bought from a pet shop is unlikely to be of a high enough quality, many shows do have classes for the novice exhibitor. In these classes the judges give points for a healthy hamster rather than for fur quality and colour distribution. Whilst there may be classes for hamsters in local pet shows the serious exhibitor will be showing at those run under the auspices of the National Hamster Council (NHC) in the UK.

The NHC is the governing body controlling the regional clubs and laying down the show rules and breed standards. They issue a monthly magazine which gives details of shows and other information. Visiting these shows to examine winning hamsters and to watch the judging are important preliminaries to beginning your show career. It is from the people exhibiting at these shows that you should try to purchase the stock for your own strain of show animals.

The first prerequisite of an exhibition hamster is that it should be tame and used to being handled. Secondly the hamster should be used to being brushed, with a cat grooming brush, although some exhibitors prefer to use a grooming box. This is a well ventilated box such as a 5 litre (2 gallon) ice cream container, filled with soft wood sawdust and hay into which the hamster will burrow and groom itself. A final shine can be applied to the coat with a 'silk' handkerchief.

On the day of the show the hamster is transferred to a standard show cage which contains only white sawdust as a flooring. The animals will be judged in these cages.

The NHC standards state that a judge should be looking for 'a hamster of good size with a broad, rounded skull on a large head, and with a short blunt, un-ratlike face. Ears should be large, set well apart and upstanding when the hamster is awake. The fur should be soft, short and dense, except in the case of longhaired hamsters. In the longhaired variety the hair should be long, soft and fine in texture.' Points are awarded in the following categories: colour, marking, fur, size, condition, ears and eyes. The perfect hamster will gain 100 points.

Index